Dyslexia and Parents.

By Margaret Malpas.
Edited by Deborah Avington.

Published by
The British Dyslexia Association
Unit 8 Bracknell Beeches, Old Bracknell Lane, Bracknell, RG12 7BW

Helpline: 0845 251 9002
Administration: 0845 251 9003
Website: **www.bdadyslexia.org.uk**

Cover design and illustrations by Dianne Giblin
www.diannegiblin.wordpress.com
Enquiries for Dianne Giblin can be made via **admin@bdadyslexia.org.uk**

D1512651

ACC. No: 02854310

ISBN 978-1-872653-56-3

9 781872 653563

British Dyslex!a
Association

Editorial Note

The views expressed in this book are those of the individual contributors, and do not necessarily represent the policy of the British Dyslexia Association.

The BDA does not endorse the advertisements included in this publication.

Whilst every effort has been made to ensure the accuracy of information given in this handbook, the BDA cannot accept responsibility for the consequences of any errors or omissions in that information.

In certain articles the masculine pronoun is used purely for the sake of convenience.

British Dyslexia Association
978-1-872653-56-3

Published in Great Britain 2012.
Copyright © British Dyslexia Association 2012.

Printed by Berforts Information Press Ltd, Oxford, UK
www.informationpress.com

Advertising sales by Space Marketing.
Tel: 01892-677-740
Fax: 01892-677-743
Email: **brians@spacemarketing.co.uk**

British Dyslexia Association.

Unit 8, Bracknell Beeches, Old Bracknell Lane, Bracknell RG12 7BW

Helpline: 0845-251-9002
Administration: 0845-251-9003
Fax: 0845-251-9005

Website: **www.bdadyslexia.org.uk**

BDA is a company limited by guarantee, registered in England No. 1830587

Registered Charity No. 289243

"Dislexser".

I was born with it
But because of it
I got hit for it
I cried about it
Fought because of it
Tried to get rid of it
Albert Einstein had it
Sulked about it
Called names because of it
I didn't like it
Mum had enough of me because of it
Couldn't be bothered to live with it
Do we really have to have it?
Mum thought I was lazy because of it
I thought I was crazy because of it
Punched walls because of it
Got in trouble over it
Disrupted class because of it
Walked out, away from it
Embarrassed because of it
I'm ashamed of it
I swore at teachers because of it
Just have to live with it

John Rogers and Lea Bourne.

Foreword.

This book has been written to help you enable your children to develop to their full potential. It contains lots of practical tips but also tries to give a comprehensive account of the theory ~ what dyslexia is, what causes it, how we learn, the role of self-esteem and so on.

It covers a very wide age range from early childhood to young adulthood. It is hoped that you will find it a useful book to dip into as your child develops through all the normal stages.

When you find that your bright five year old is having difficulty with reading, which is what often triggers the first thoughts that something is not quite right, it is an emotional time. The author has tried to acknowledge this emotional response in the book and hopes that you will find some comfort and answers here too.

Dyslexia never goes away but with the right support, your dyslexic child can achieve greatly and will have special gifts that will bring you much pleasure and pride.

About the Author.

Margaret Malpas is the proud mum of two young adults, one of whom is dyslexic. She is also a qualified specialist teacher in dyslexia and has over 25 years of experience in training others, particularly through supported open learning.

Acknowledgements and thanks.

There is substantial material in the book which has been provided by the BDA Helpline and Helen Boden (Training Manager, Accreditation at BDA). Thanks are gratefully given for their expertise, support and the material they have provided here.

Contents.

Chapter 1 – What is Dyslexia?

One of the inevitable questions for the parent of a child with dyslexia is why? Why is my child dyslexic? We will try to answer this question in this chapter where we will be looking at what dyslexia is and why some people have it and others don't. We will also be examining the strengths and weaknesses that some dyslexic individuals have. We can't pretend that finding your child may be dyslexic may not be a worrying time but remember there has been tremendous progress in the last twenty years in understanding the condition. There are now a range of solutions to the problems it can present and it is recognised that people with dyslexia may have unusual and helpful strengths. So, be optimistic, in reading this, you are well on the way to addressing any issues. First, however, we need to see it from our position as parents.

The role we have as parents.

Most parents want the best for their children. This, perhaps, is better expressed as:

Their goal is to:

> "bring their children up to become fully functioning, independent adults who have developed to their full potential."

Parenthood can be a pretty bumpy ride at times and for the parents of a child with learning differences, this can bring particular, though surmountable, difficulties. One of the things we need to clarify is the role that parents can and should play in the development of their dyslexic child. You might find it helpful to think about the following things:

- Protecting, feeding and clothing your child
- Choosing an appropriate school for your child
- Knowing what your child is entitled to and fighting for it
- Loving your child and providing a stable family background
- Teaching your child
- Building your child's self esteem
- Encouraging moral development
- Passing on your values and attitudes

All these are things good parents do. However, they don't do all of them alone. For example, teaching children and encouraging moral development is also part of the child's school role. What often happens with a dyslexic child is that the parent has to take on some of the responsibility for the teaching role. For example, the parent may have to be more involved in helping the child to read than they would with a child who is not dyslexic, or they may have to be more 'hands on' in developing the child's self-esteem than they would otherwise have deemed necessary. This is a balancing act though, as it is not normally practical to teach a child at home if you also have to earn a living. Additionally, it is important that the child learns to become independent and there are dangers in being too pushy, over controlling or not giving your child space to grow.

As we look at different aspects of helping your dyslexic child, your role will be discussed too. Meanwhile, we need to first determine what it is we're dealing with, that is, what is dyslexia?

Dyslexia is often thought of as being a problem with word recognition. However, it is a syndrome of learning differences which can include problems with literacy. It is a genetically inherited condition and we know that it is much more common than we thought. It is also what is called a co-occurring condition. That means that there are a whole range of aspects of the condition that are differently labelled but they all come from the same root. So we have conditions like dyslexia, which is how we label difficulties with becoming fully literate, or dyscalculia, which is what we call it when someone has difficulties learning arithmetic. However, every person with any of these conditions is likely to have some bits from one condition and some from another. This means that everyone who is labelled as being dyslexic actually presents slightly different symptoms.

Some people only have very mild symptoms whilst others are severely dyslexic. Some dyslexic individuals have very well developed creative and interpersonal skills, others have strong oral skills. Some are not exceptional in any way but all have strengths. The key is to develop those strengths and mitigate any weaknesses.

But why are some people dyslexic?

There are many theories around what dyslexia is and new research is emerging on a regular basis.

Current thinking would indicate that there are differences within the brain of a dyslexic person and that these are genetically based so dyslexia is generally inherited. In many families you can see clear evidence of this where one or both parents has similar difficulties from one or more of their children. We also know that if the father is dyslexic, then there is a considerable chance that his sons will also be dyslexic.

Research using modern brain scanning equipment has shown that the brains of dyslexic individuals are different, particularly in the way that the signals pass between the different parts of the brain. It is this difference in transmission that is responsible for some of the challenges which dyslexic individuals face, but it is also responsible for some of the strengths they have too.

Many theories have emerged to try to explain how a dyslexic individual's thought processes may differ in response to the physical differences in the brain. However, most of these theories have concentrated on the problems that the differences cause rather than the positive aspects. A good way to think of it is that dyslexic people are just different, they process things slightly differently and what we need to do is respond to that difference.

Fortunately, we have come a long way in recent years and dyslexia is now generally recognized - it is no longer denied. Most people have heard of it, although they often do not understand what it is or how it affects those who have it. Many teachers and schools now are aware of the condition but we are still a long way from all teachers understanding it fully or knowing how to teach pupils with dyslexia. That is why this book is so important, parents need to know as much as possible to be able to pass on knowledge and get the very best support for their children.

What are the effects of dyslexia?

What follows is a general description and you need to note that not all dyslexic individuals will be affected in the same way or to the same level.

One definitive feature of dyslexia, , is that it affects each individual in different ways. Its effects can also be magnified or reduced depending on what the person is trying to do and the level of stress they are under. We know that the difficulties dyslexia throws up are definitely worse when the person is stressed. There are also times when an individual will have good days and bad days in terms of performance, a task that seemed easy yesterday, may seem difficult today. This on/off, temporal effect can be very confusing for parents and teachers alike.

Strengths.

Dyslexic individuals process information differently from others and although they may have difficulties with words, the very differences in brain structure that cause such difficulties, also lead to improved performance in other areas such as:

- The ability to visualise things
- Practical and problem solving skills
- Lateral thinking skills
- Being able to see the big picture (global thinkers) in terms of strategies and problem solving
- Good visual-spatial awareness
- Creativity and the ability to think "outside the box"

- Good verbal communication skills
- High levels of motivation and persistence

Some dyslexic individuals regard their dyslexia as a gift because it gives them a very different view on life and so many compensatory skills. There are numerous examples of very gifted individuals who were or are dyslexic ranging from Albert Einstein to Winston Churchill to Steve Redgrave, Olympic gold winner, to Billy Connelly, comedian. It does appear to be more common in boys but there are examples of famous women too who are dyslexic such as Kara Tointon and Whoopi Goldberg.

There is a high incidence of entrepreneurs who are dyslexic. According to Baum's study, 33% of students with learning difficulties are gifted (Baum 1985). Therefore, although we tend to concentrate on the difficulties dyslexic individuals have in our very literate world, it is important to realise that if we can resolve some of their difficulties with literacy, we may unleash great talent.

Specific weaknesses.

Unfortunately we cannot pretend that dyslexia doesn't cause some difficulties but as you read this, remember that there are lots of ways around the weaknesses we are describing here. You will find out about these as you go further into the book. First it is necessary for you to gain an understanding of some of the technical issues so you can see how the coping skills and developmental strategies offered later can be used or modified by you and your child.

There are four areas relating to dyslexia which cause specific weaknesses. These are:

Difficulties with processing visual information effectively.

Some individuals have a difficulty with their visual memory i.e. remembering what they have seen, which can also affect the ability to learn to read and spell. There are many words within the English language which we have to learn by sight alone, particularly the little words e.g. was, and, so, the, that have little meaning but are vital in sentence structure. However, not all individuals with dyslexia have this difficulty and many find that their visual memory is a positive strength.

Some people with dyslexia (and others who are not dyslexic too) find that words on paper move around so that when reading or writing anything the process becomes very difficult. Some will also report that objects move around, for example when they try to catch a ball it appears to move erratically, making it virtually impossible to see where it will land and therefore where you should put your hands to catch it. You might have noticed that at an early age, your child had difficulty learning to catch things. This is because they have a visual distraction. Fortunately this can easily be rectified by the use of coloured filters (more later.)

Being able to process sounds effectively.

If you are unable to distinguish between similar sounds, which is a problem within the brain not the ears, this can have a considerable impact on your ability to learn to read and spell effectively. It can make it difficult to take apart and put together the sounds in words. Sometimes, the aural memory is affected and this can make it difficult to find the word that you want to say. It can also affect the process of storing and retrieving information that you hear.

Memory.

This is the ability to remember information effectively in both short term and working memory and the ability to develop some skills to a level where they become automatic. Memory can be broken down into three parts:

1. Short term memory: this takes in information and holds it for a short time. An average adult can remember 7 digits in a string + or – 2 (so anywhere between 5 and 9 is standard).

2. Working memory: this is where we are able to process new information. It is very critical when we are learning to be able to manipulate pictures, sounds, ideas. For example, when we are learning to spell we need to hold the word and manipulate it into our longer term memory. We also use our working memory as a search engine to retrieve a word from our long-term memory storage.

3. Long term memory: this is like the filing cabinet where information is stored long term.

All of the above processes are being used all of the time; dyslexic individuals tend to experience difficulties in short term and/or working memory.

Speed of processing of the brain.

Lots of people with dyslexia suffer from a slight slowing down of the speed at which the brain works. This is may be an insignificant slowing down but the more information they have to process, or the more pressure they are under the slower the processing of the brain and it may then be perceptible. This is generally due to the way the brain is "wired" and whilst this can be responsible for much more creative thinking, it also can be responsible for this slight slowing down.

How does it feel to be dyslexic?

Dyslexic individuals have very different symptoms and strengths so there probably isn't one way of describing what it feels like. As dyslexia occurs across a range, with some individuals barely affected, some moderately affected and others more profoundly affected, their experiences will differ. Some people find that their biggest challenge is coping with a weaker working memory. Others find it difficult to concentrate on the task in hand, whilst others may say that coping with organising their lives is the biggest hurdle. Really, everyone is different in their response to this inherited condition. We've given different names to the condition according to how it mainly manifests itself.

We call it dyslexia when the most common difficulty experienced is with literacy. Given the knowledge of how to teach those with dyslexia, it can still often take more persistence and effort to gain reading and writing skills. Sometimes, even when these have been acquired to a reasonable level, there can still be persistent problems relating to speed, understanding what has been read, fluency of reading, spelling, written expression etc. Spelling is often the skill that is less easy to remediate, but as we now have spell checkers on all computers, this is a good example of how we learn to cope where things are difficult to accomplish.

Weaknesses within the memory systems can also cause problems with organisation, sequencing, remembering messages, lists of instructions, handling information that requires using a sequence of data etc.

Regarding problems with numeracy, we call it dyscalculia when it is the processes and procedures of making calculations, recognising/confusing symbols and remembering times tables which pose problems, rather than understanding the concepts.

Difficulties can be found for some within the area of social interaction, and this may be referred to as mild Aspergers Syndrome. Also remembering names, finding the correct label for something, saying the wrong thing in the wrong tone, confusing words and phrases e.g. par cark for car park can lead to embarrassment and a fear of saying the wrong or inappropriate thing. It can make an individual appear "slow" in their interactions with others as they may need more time to process incoming information.

We need to recognise the child's difficulties as early as possible so that we can help them, as they can cause an impact on someone's life if ignored. It is going to be difficult if you can only buy the products you recognize. How can you eat out in a restaurant if you can't read a menu? How can you travel to somewhere new if you can't read the signs or understand a bus or a train timetable? We can usually do something about all these things, reasonably easily, with just a bit of extra support.

Unfortunately in the past, dyslexia wasn't accepted or recognised and most people didn't get any help. Many older people with dyslexia have found that they later lacked confidence and self-esteem, and they may also react with anger or frustration. We want to avoid any of these negative emotions. We need to make sure that children and young people with dyslexia or a related condition focus on their individual strengths and the things they *can* do.

In the next chapter, we are going to look at the more positive aspects of how you spot dyslexia and then what you can do about it. However, first here is a brief overview of the chapter which will help some people, especially if they are dyslexic, to grasp the content.

Summary.

In this chapter the key points were:

- You will need to think about your role as a parent and what you are going to try to achieve
- Dyslexia is a processing issue, it affects the way we take in and manipulate information
- There are four particular weaknesses it presents – both visual and auditory processing of information, working memory issues and slower processing speed of the brain
- All dyslexic individuals have a different range of strengths and weaknesses
- Dyslexia can affect many aspects of one's life and its effect on one's self esteem is critical
- Many dyslexic individuals are exceptionally successful adults
- We need to help dyslexic children recognise and use their strengths and minimise the effects of any weaknesses
- Dyslexia brings some special talents and it's not the end!

Chapter 2 – Spotting Dyslexia.

Unless you or your partner is dyslexic, it is only when your child starts school and they do not learn to read as quickly as others in their class, that you may suspect something is not quite right. However, there are signs in young children that may give clues to the presence of dyslexia. The earlier it is recognised the better as you can start to help your child with strategies which will help them to overcome some of the difficulties.

Equally importantly, although you may suspect that your child is dyslexic, they might not be and the correct identification is very important.

Here are some specific signs of dyslexia which you may recognise at the different stages of development.

Pre-school children may show:

- Persistent difficulty in learning nursery rhymes or the name for things, like "table" or "chair"
- Enjoyment in being read to but no interest in letters or words
- Signs of apparently not paying attention
- Continuing difficulties in getting dressed efficiently and putting shoes on the correct feet
- Problems with catching, kicking or throwing a ball or with hopping or skipping
- Difficulty with clapping a simple rhythm
- Delayed speech development

Primary school children may show:

- A poor sense of direction and confuse left and right
- Difficulty tying shoe laces and dressing
- A discrepancy between receptive and expressive language
- Short-term memory limitations, for instance, finding it hard to remember arithmetic tables, the alphabet or classroom instructions

- Pronounced reading difficulties – but don't forget that not all dyslexic children have these problems. Specifically look out for:

  ○ Hesitant or laboured reading

  ○ Omitted lines or repetition of the same line – loss of place in the text

  ○ Muddling words that look alike, e.g. "no" and "on," "for" and "off" and "was" and "saw"

  ○ Difficulties in saying multi-syllabic words

  ○ Problems understanding what they have read

- Difficulties with writing and spelling. Errors might include:

  ○ A disparity between written and spoken language

  ○ Messy work, for example, curled pages, crossings out and badly set out

  ○ Handwriting that looks heavy and laborious - Confusion of similar letters, like "b" and "d", "p" and "q" and "w" and "m" – resulting in some bizarre spelling

  ○ The same word spelt differently in the same piece of work such as "more", "mor" and "mro" – confusion between upper and lower case letters, and concepts of letter, name and sound

Secondary school pupils may:

- Still read inaccurately
- Still have problems with spelling
- Confuse places, times and dates
- Have difficulty remembering maths tables and formulae
- Need to have instructions repeated
- Get "tied up" using long words, such as "preliminary" or "philosophical"
- Have difficulty planning and writing essays
- Suffer poor confidence and low self-esteem

As a parent you will be aware of some of this but some things may not be so obvious when the problem occurs in school. Secondary school offers a new set of challenges which can place immense pressure on pupils with dyslexia, who may already have problems with their short-term memory and organisational skills. This may demonstrate itself in:

- Forgetting which books to bring to class
- Difficulty organising life around a timetable
- Misunderstanding complex instructions
- Problems trying to write down notes at speed, and completing work on time
- Memory difficulties which affect the marshalling of learned facts effectively in exams.

You may only find out about these difficulties in conversations with your child's teacher. In addition, your child may cope in the early years but find it increasingly difficult to manage when the workload becomes more demanding as they get older. This is why we see pupils getting identified as dyslexic when they start to do GCSE's or even later. However, when your child starts to find it more difficult to cope, you may notice that, as a result of the strain, they may return from school extremely tired and fractious. They may employ avoidance techniques, such as saying they don't want to go to school or in the worst cases, truanting. It is easy to see how motivation and self esteem drop rapidly. For some children these manifest themselves in challenging behaviour either for you as a parent or at school.

September 2012

mon	Tues	wed	Thurs	Frid	Sat	Sun
					1	2
3	4	5	6	7	8	9
10	11	12	13	14	15	16
17 18	25	19	26 20	21	22	23
24			27	28	29	30

What if it's not dyslexia?

It is important to remember that each child is an individual and is therefore likely to have a different pattern of both strengths and difficulties. It is normal with dyslexia for there to be an array of indicators from the lists above. Their abilities will also be influenced not only by the severity of their dyslexia but also by how much support they have had. However, some of the issues that dyslexia presents could also be due to other causes.

■ Inadequate education.

If a child has had limited opportunity to access appropriate education then it would not be surprising that their literacy levels may be lower than expected. We sometimes see this in children who have had several stays in hospital at a critical point in learning to read.

■ Broken or disrupted education.

If a child has encountered frequent changes in education such as changes of school it may also result in lower than expected literacy levels. It usually takes a child most of the first term to settle into a new school (a bit like when you start a new job).

■ Disrupted emotional background.

If there has been a lot of change within the family which the child has had difficulty coping with, then again this may have had an impact on the child in terms of them being less receptive to education for a period due to emotional upheaval. We see this sometimes with children who have been bereaved.

■ Children with lower ability levels.

A small proportion of the general population has lower ability levels. However, the proportion who are unable to learn to read and write is very small and these are generally regarded as having an IQ score below 80 so it is fairly rare. Secondary school pupils who are of lower ability may exhibit indicators that are similar to those of dyslexia, for example, poor literacy/numeracy skills and difficulty with acquiring work related skills. Individuals can be of lower ability and also dyslexic, of course.

■ Individuals who have suffered a brain injury.

In some circumstances damage to the brain sustained through an injury or trauma can also present in similar ways to dyslexia.

■ Young people who have a history of long term substance abuse.

A history of long-term substance abuse may affect an individual's cognitive (thought processing) skills and being on drugs currently can affect the individual's ability to learn.

■ Other physical difficulty.

Before continuing with any screening for dyslexia, it is always advisable to rule out any other physical factors such as previously undiagnosed problems with hearing, such as glue ear, or eyesight.

If these tell-tale signs suggest to you that your child is dyslexic, then ideally this should trigger an assessment, preferably from a specialist dyslexia teacher in the school. However, this often isn't available and for those with mild to moderate dyslexia, some adjustments in their education may be enough. A good understanding of their difficulties and strengths should help you discuss what needs to be done with your child's teacher. If they continue to fall behind, however, they should be fast tracked to more specialist assessment and support.

Typically, the child is first observed in the classroom, then if the teacher has some concerns they will try some adjustments to their teaching. For example, they may give them more targeted support in learning the sounds of letters or teaching new concepts through more frequent rehearsal to make sure they are fully embedded in their long term memory. If this doesn't work, they may decide to screen for dyslexia and then ultimately, the child may need a full diagnostic assessment of their strengths and weaknesses. A description of screening and diagnosis follows next.

Screening.

Here is a brief description of screening and identification techniques. It is given so that you know what is available. It is not appropriate for you to undertake your own screening of your child.

The issue of the identification of dyslexia can be a thorny issue. You may find that the school considers their resources to be fully stretched, is not very keen to encourage screening if the difficulties are mild and it is felt that they can easily be addressed in the classroom. Nonetheless, the earlier dyslexia is picked up the better, as your child can be taught appropriately and is less likely to fall behind. The following table gives a brief overview of the different screening and assessments used.

Screening methods table.

Identification Method	Description	When would it be used	Advantages	Disadvantages
Checklists	A simple list of questions that give an indication of dyslexia, e.g. the B.D.A. checklist.	This can be done by an individual, can be a useful first step in identification.	Individuals can do it on their own, in private. It is quick and usually non-threatening.	The questions asked might not be relevant to everyone. Gives only an indication .
Screening	A more detailed series of activities that examine key areas.	This can be used by a non-specialist and will give an indication of the probability of dyslexia.	Gives a more accurate result, can identify areas of more specific difficulty and is relatively quick.	The tools are only as good as the person using them.
Dyslexia Specialist Assessment	Usually uses a variety of tools to produce a picture of strengths and difficulties, and a more detailed report.	Usually used in an educational context to identify specific support strategies.	Specialist knowledge should produce an accurate result with quality recommendations for support, (including exam concessions).	Such an assessment can take a long time and be more costly.
Psychological Assessment	Variety of tests used to see how an individual processes information indicating strengths and difficulties.	Usually used in an educational or employment context, to provide the most accurate identification of dyslexia.	Vital where there are issues of litigation.	Can take a long time and is costly. The results can sometimes be difficult to interpret.

How are Children Assessed?

If the child does not respond to additional support and alternative approaches within the classroom, or if severe dyslexia is suspected, then they should have a full diagnostic assessment. Unfortunately, this is not routinely done and there can be a postcode lottery element to it. In some areas, local education authorities have invested in creating specialist teams within the county but this is not the case everywhere, and many of those teams are now being disbanded as LEAs reduce their budgets. There is no funding available for these assessments when they are done privately. They take a lot of time and have to be undertaken by a specialist, so we anticipate a fee of hundreds of pounds to get a private assessment.

What do we mean by assessment?

When there are concerns about your child's progress in literacy or arithmetic, or with their social interaction, class teachers, often with a Special Educational Needs Co-ordinator (SENCo) and Teaching Assistants, who know your child well, begin by building up a profile of strengths and weaknesses. These assessments look at how children perform with certain tasks . They can be quick to use and most can be administered in the classroom rather than making an issue of withdrawing the pupil into another room. Check sheets can be used for recording such information. A checklist of areas of difficulty which a teacher will use might be as follows:

Observational Checklist.

Discrepancies in intelligence/attainment.

- Oral/written word
- Within National Curriculum subjects
- Between National Curriculum subjects
- Understanding/memory for facts
- Good days/bad days
- Effort put in/quality of end result

Language processing difficulties.

- Mishearing
- Difficulty following simple instructions
- Difficulty saying polysyllabic words
- Difficulty with rhyme
- Difficulty segmenting sounds
- Difficulty blending sounds
- Problem with labelling: Right/left, up/down, names
- Word-finding difficulties
- Convoluted explanations
- Playing for time: "ums, ahs"
- Poor or confused knowledge of letter names/sounds
- Erratic spelling
- Avoiding writing and spelling
- Poor syntax and punctuation
- Poor basic reading
- Poor comprehension
- Difficulty reading music

Working Memory Difficulties.

- Copying from blackboard or notes
- Making notes/taking dictation
- Remembering facts/formulae
- Poor sense of direction
- Remembering instructions/messages

Slow speed of Language processing

* Takes/needs longer to process information when listening/ speaking and particularly when multi-tasking

  ○ Reading

  ○ Writing

  ○ Spelling

Checklists or performance indicators can provide a valuable source of information in any assessment process. They are helpful in building a picture of a child's strengths and weaknesses and as a starting point of ways to help the child in the classroom. Checklists do not *diagnose* dyslexia or other specific difficulties.

A specialist teacher may be able to pinpoint patterns of strengths and weakness or characteristics that would suggest the possibility of dyslexia.

If it is decided that the pupil's difficulties are persistent to the extent that they are not making the expected progress in learning, then a more standardised form of assessment may need to be carried out. Detailed assessments can be carried out by specialist teachers (with a qualification such as the Diploma in Assessing and Teaching those with Dyslexia, or Associate Member of the British Dyslexia Association (AMBDA) status) or by a chartered psychologist.

What does a psychologist look for?

The purpose of an assessment is to discover whether the pupil is failing and if the pupil is falling behind expected levels of performance. It is important to establish whether this is because of:

- *overall* low ability
- sensory impairment (vision/hearing problems)
- motor problems
- repeated absence from school due to illness
- emotional or social factors such as family problems, poor self-image, lack of motivation
- frequent changes of school, lack of early schooling
- English as a second language
- or whether the pupil has a **specific learning difficulty**

As already mentioned, it is important to consider a pupil's strengths as well as weaknesses when assessing them.

An educational psychologist assessment.

The aim of the assessment is to build a detailed picture of both the child's strengths and weaknesses and to identify whether there is a pattern to these that could be consistent with a diagnosis of a specific learning difficulty.

In order to do this the psychologist will gather a range of information from a variety of sources. This might include reports from teachers, SENCos, Teaching Assistants and parents or carers. Parents should be asked to either complete a questionnaire or meet with the psychologist to discuss the

patoss

The Professional Association
of Teachers of Students with
Specific learning difficulties

Patoss - The largest professional association for SpLD Specialist Teachers in the UK

Patoss is one of the largest providers of tutors who work with students with specific learning difficulties across the age ranges from primary to adults.

Many of our members are qualified assessors who are able to carry out a range of assesments including assessing for support programs, access arrangements and Disabled Student Allowances.

Patoss has a network of local groups across the country providing events which you may be able to attend.

Information about Patoss and assessors, tutors and local groups can be found on our website www.patoss-dyslexia.org or phone 01386 712650, or email patoss@sworcs.ac.uk

child. The areas that are covered within either questionnaires or discussions might include issues associated with the general health of the child such as medical history, for example any medication that is regularly taken, e.g. for asthma, etc., frequent occurrences of illness such as ear infections or associated conditions such as glue ear.

They may also ask about the child's birth such as whether it was a normal or assisted delivery and whether or not the child reached the usual developmental milestones (walking, talking, etc) within the expected time frame. They should also discuss with parents their view of the child's difficulties from both an educational perspective and within the home environment; this should also include aspects of behaviour such as self-esteem, frustration, aggression, etc.

Finally in this process, as you might be able to provide useful information about your son or daughter that the school is unaware, it is important that you participate fully and that this will assist the Educational Psychologist in their assessment.

Assessment via a Specialist Teacher.

Specialist teachers have done at least a year's extra study, and often eighteen months, to gain additional qualifications so that they can assess individuals who may be dyslexic. They will follow the same process as a psychologist in carrying out an assessment. The only differences are that the specialist teacher's training is more specific to teaching and so they use a specific battery of tests. They are not qualified to diagnose or give advice upon conditions other than dyslexia and its related conditions. For example, if the child has ADHD (attention deficit disorder with hyperactivity), the specialist teacher may well spot this but would have to recommend that this is investigated further as they are not qualified to assess it. However, the specialist teacher usually knows much more about current teaching practices and will probably make recommendations that are easier for parents to follow at a practical level. Their services are generally cheaper than that of a psychologist who has undergone training for many more years.

What is analysed in the full diagnostic assessment?

The first thing that will be looked at is **underlying ability**, also known as IQ or in other words, what the child might be expected to achieve. This is usually measured using a set of tests ranging over verbal and non-verbal skills. So that you recognise what is in a report if you have your child assessed, the most commonly used tests by UK psychologists are the WISC and the BAS. A specialist teacher needs to be trained to level 7 (or has AMBDA certification) to carry out this testing and if so will use the Wide Range Intelligence Test (WRIT). There are specific things in these tests which enable the assessor to see underlying deficits which are typical of a dyslexia profile. This is why these tests are important, although understanding what a child's general level of ability should be is also very useful.

The next area for investigation is **educational attainment;** how well is the child doing in reading, spelling and numeracy skills? The pupil should be able to perform as well in these as his underlying ability suggests. If the pupil performs very poorly in the areas of attainment then there is what we call a discrepancy. This means that there is an unexpected gap between his IQ test score and his actual levels of achievement. Therefore, something is preventing him from achieving his true performance levels.

The psychologist or specialist teacher will need to pinpoint the reasons for this discrepancy, and they will do this by the means of **diagnostic testing**. We have already considered the areas of learning that characterise dyslexia, so the psychologist or specialist teacher will test the child's ability in these areas of classic weakness:

- Language processing
- Memory
- Speed of processing

Differential Diagnosis

These concentric circles are a very helpful way to look at a discrepancy model:

The assessment is a very detailed process and usually lasts for anything up to 3 hours. Parents are not usually encouraged to be with the child whilst the assessment is taking place.

The test results:

Following the assessment the psychologist or specialist teacher will produce a written report of their findings and they may also give you verbal feedback.

The written report will contain both the scores from the tests and recommendations for future support.

The test scores can appear confusing as they are often presented as "standard scores" and/or "percentile rank". This is because a psychologist or specialist teacher uses tests that are standardised, i.e. they compare like with like, when a child is tested, for example, on reading. There is a level that a child of the same age would be expected to score; if your child scores below this level then they might be below average, if they score above this level then they might be above average. The exact average score for a "standard score" is 100 and the exact average score for "percentile rank" is 50, however, very few people would score exactly on this midway point so these scores are further split into bands that indicate whether, or not they are within the average range. This can be very helpful for you as a parent as you can see how your child compares against average markers and can use the descriptors, such as above average etc.

Descriptive Category	Standard Score	Percentile Rank
Lower Extreme	69 and below	2 and below
Well Below Average	70 - 79	3 – 8
Below Average	80 – 89	9 – 24
Average	90 – 109	25 – 74
Above Average	110 - 119	75 – 90
Well Above Average	120 - 129	91 – 97
Upper Extreme	130 and above	98 and above

A dyslexic child's scores will often be inconsistent, for example, scoring within the average range for IQ but within the below or well below average ranges for reading and spelling. This pattern of performance would indicate discrepancies or differences and, depending on where such differences occur, could present a pattern that is consistent with that expected for dyslexia or other specific learning difficulties. Based on the scale of such differences psychologists and specialist teachers can then also indicate the severity of the difficulties, for example, mild, moderate or severe and pin point exactly where the difficulties arise.

It should be noted that few psychologists will give a definitive diagnosis and are likely to word the summary of their findings in terms such as "a pattern of difficulties that could be consistent with a specific learning difficulty such as dyslexia". A specialist teacher may be more likely to say that the child is dyslexic.

Recommendations:

The final report should contain recommendations of support (if appropriate). They should include those that the school can implement, those that you can do as parents and possibly suggestions for specialist support which you may need to access privately.

So what do I do if I suspect my child is dyslexic?

If after reading all this, you suspect that your child is dyslexic, this is what you can do as a next step.

If your child is not yet at school there are some suggestions for useful ideas in later chapters which can help to strengthen their abilities in areas that will become important when they go to school. You can make these into games which you both enjoy.

If your child is already at school, then you will need to talk to the staff about providing suitable help and support. If the school has a good understanding of dyslexia and adequate funding, it may not be necessary to go through all the stages below. In other cases, you may need to take a more active approach to get the help you need. You should always discuss with the school what you intend to do – because in the end it is the school which will have to implement any action plan.

1. Speak to the class teacher (primary) or head of year (secondary).

2. Contact your local dyslexia association (details of how to do this are included at the end of this book).

3. Make an appointment with the Special Educational Needs Coordinator (SENCo).

4. Ask for a plan which details your child's targets and the support they are receiving.

5. Get an assessment by an educational psychologist or specialist teacher.

6. Discuss the assessment report with the school.

1. Speak to the class teacher (primary) or head of year (secondary).

Tell them about your concerns and why you think your child might be dyslexic. They may be able to identify and provide support that your child needs.

2. Contact your local dyslexia association.

The British Dyslexia Association (B.D.A.) has a helpline on 0845-251-9002 and a website at **www.bdadyslexia.org.uk** from which you can get more information including contact details for your Local Dyslexia Association. This can provide you with information about support that is available in the local area.

3. Make an appointment with the Special Educational Needs Coordinator (SENCo) at your child's school.

After a meeting with the class teacher or head of year, if you still have concerns, you should make an appointment to see the school SENCo.

There is a raft of legislation, including the Equality Act (2010) that provides rights for children with disabilities such as dyslexia. Therefore, your child is entitled to appropriate teaching and support if they are encountering these kind of difficulties. A word of warning here though. If your child has mild difficulties, what is called "quality first teaching" is seen as sufficient for their needs to be catered for within the classroom. Secondly, whilst your child's teachers will really want to help, they may not have had adequate training to do so and the school may say it does not have the resources to provide individual support.

It is advisable to contact the B.D.A. Helpline (email: **helpline@bdadyslexia.org.uk** or phone 0845-251-9002) if you are beginning to feel your child is not getting the support they need. We also regularly update advisory sheets on our website and these set out the rights parents and children have and explain procedures.

4. Plan of targets and support for your child.

The school should establish a plan of what your child should be able to achieve in the term and what support they need. You should expect to have regular meetings with the school (perhaps once a term) to monitor progress. If all goes well, your child should now receive appropriate help and support.

If, however, this plan is not working or, for some reason, is not properly implemented, it may be necessary to get a full assessment by a psychologist, or a specialist teacher.

5. Getting an assessment by an educational psychologist.

You could request that an educational psychologist at the Local Education Authority (LA) does a formal assessment. If the school is unwilling to refer your child, you can apply for this yourself directly or get help from the Parent Partnership Officer at the LA.

The LA service is often over-stretched and there may be a long waiting list. Several LAs also have a budget for assessments and so they tend to be rationed for the children with the most severe problems (not just in dyslexia but all other disabilities and difficulties) So, if you can afford it, you could consider having a private assessment done either by a suitably qualified teacher or a Chartered Educational Psychologist specialising in Specific Learning Difficulties. This would cost from £375 and would give you a full written report with recommendations for educational support, as described previously.

You can find information on psychologists from the British Psychological Society's website, at **www.bps.org.uk**.

The B.D.A. can also recommend psychologists for you in independent assessment centres.

If you want to find a specialist teacher, then there are several sources:

(a) You can get a list of specialist teachers with AMBDA (Associate member status) or ATS (Approved teacher status) from the B.D.A. These teachers have done a course which the B.D.A. has accredited and have experience which they have verified. You can get this list by emailing **accreditation@bdadyslexia.org.uk**.

(b) The Patoss organisation also has a list of specialist teachers (with or without B.D.A. accreditation).

(c) Dyslexia Action and Helen Arkell centres also provide specialist teacher assessments.

6. Discuss the assessment report with the school.

Once you have an assessment, meet with the SENCo and discuss the findings of the report. The report should form the basis for an action plan to help your child.

If you obtain an independent assessment, however, the school may not automatically accept the findings. In this case, you should contact the Chief Education Officer for your Local Authority and ask him or her to ensure that the school implements an action plan.

If you continue to have difficulty getting the school to provide adequate support, you may need to enlist the help of the school governor in charge of Special Needs. With a diagnosed disability, your child could be entitled to support under the Disability Discrimination legislation at school.

Summary.

In this chapter, the following points have been discussed:

- How to spot the tell-tale signs of dyslexia
- What else it might be
- How assessment is done and what happens next
- What to do next if you suspect your child is dyslexic:
    1. Speak to the class teacher (primary or head of year (secondary).
    2. Contact your local dyslexia association (details of how to do this are included at the end of this book.)

3. Make an appointment with the Special Educational Needs Coordinator.

4. Get a plan with targets and support for your child established.

5. Get an assessment by an educational psychologist.

6. Discuss the assessment report with the school

Chapter 3 – What you can do to help your child.

In addition to all the usual parenting activities there are five ways in which you can specifically help your child and some of these cannot be done by anyone else. They are:

1. Building your child's self esteem
2. Determining the best strategy for your child's education
3. Building good partnerships with your child's school and teachers
4. Helping them develop coping mechanisms which minimise any weaknesses
5. Helping them become literate and numerate

Building your child's self esteem.

Individuals build up confidence through trying out new things, being successful and enjoying feelings of achievement. This encourages them to go on and try more new experiences and if these succeed, then their confidence grows.

The converse of this is that if an individual tries something and does not succeed, there is no afterglow of satisfaction and instead, they may feel they have failed which puts them off trying new things. This is a vicious cycle which is extremely destructive to their learning as we learn throughout our lives from new experiences and how they affect us.

If you apply this thinking to your child, you can see how trying new things at school, particularly in the area of literacy, may not be a positive experience for them. Consequently, the most helpful thing you can do for your child is to provide them with opportunities for new experiences where they can succeed and feel good about themselves. This is also an area where only you or your child's family can help. It is impossible for this to be addressed wholly in school, where there are so many children needing similar attention to their individual needs.

Secondly, we often build our own self esteem by measuring ourselves against others. It's important for our children to feel they can achieve the same things as their peers. In school they may discover that they can't read as well as their friends and because they are underachieving their self-esteem takes a knock. Additionally, we often measure ourselves against others in a pecking order, "Have I come first, second or third?" for example. Success, measured in this way, may be rare and will often reduce a perfectly good effort to be thought of as a failure - "you don't get any prizes for being fourth" syndrome.

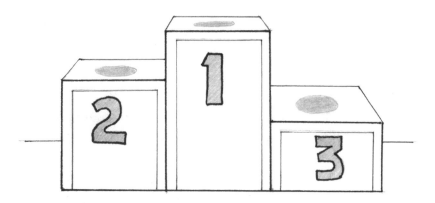

In actual fact, failure is often a necessary stage on the route to success. We need to allow our children to make mistakes, to take risks and to acknowledge that this is part of the learning process. Ask anyone who has started their own successful business and you will almost certainly find that the successful venture is the third or fourth attempt at going it alone! This is a result of the learning cycle (Kolb 1982) where we do something, then think about it, then generalise (if it works like this here, it should also work over there too) and, finally, make adjustments to what we are doing from the ideas we have formed about it. When we fail, we need to think, why did it fail, what can I learn from this about this activity? We can then improve what we are doing. It's an example of the power of positive thinking rather than the destructive potential of negative thinking which is something we will come on to a little later.

So what do we do in practice as a consequence of all this? Here are a few things you can try.

1. Look for lots of different things your child can try out so that you can find out what appeals to them. Activities organised in the school holidays can be extremely useful as they are usually arranged to be taster sessions which can later be developed into a full hobby should they appeal sufficiently. This can be especially true of sports and craft activities.

2. When they have found something they enjoy and might be good at, provide resources for the activity, including time, and encourage it. This could be really important as it might be the thing that does most to help them develop self-esteem. It is critically important that your child with dyslexia finds something they are really good at.

3. Create lots of opportunities for your child to be active, like running and climbing. Regular trips to the park and their play areas are a good idea. In part this is to release the "feel good" chemicals and also to burn off any frustration but it also helps children develop confidence in their physical abilities.

4. Recognise that there are things your child is going to have to accomplish which may be really difficult for them. For example, a great deal of sustained effort and determination will be involved in learning to read and to write legibly. So empathise with them and recognise and praise the efforts they are making.

5. Read to them, encourage a love of stories and talk about what you're reading. Make sure there are lots of pictures around the home, introduce them to the library. Use story CDs in the car, let them listen to them again when they go to bed and share with them the books that their peers are reading by themselves so that they can join in discussions about them. Take them for outings to see children's theatre or to pantomime or to hear live music. All of these things are enjoyable and will build the child's vocabulary so they are not disadvantaged even if they take longer to learn to read. It's going to be important that they value the spoken word and the arts even if they may find access a bit more difficult than children without dyslexia.

6. Talk to your child and start work on giving them positive thinking mechanisms. This will be discussed in more detail below.

Here are some things which you must **not** do.

1. Don't chastise your child because they cannot do
    something because they think and process information
    differently. For example, if they can't remember
    where their books are, then it's really not their fault.
    They will need help with strategies for organising
    and sequencing.

2. Don't discuss your worries and concerns for their future
    with family, friends or teachers within their earshot.
    You *will* need support and to talk to others but find a
    time to do it when your child is not around. Also, for
    your own sanity, choose people to support you who
    will be sympathetic and helpful and are good listeners -
    positive thinking strategies are important for you too!

3. Watch out for learned helplessness. It is important as
    parents that we give our children the chance to learn
    independence. It's important that they learn to do
    some things for themselves even if they are difficult.
    If your child is used to always having adult support
    with their homework, for example, they may develop a
    false sense of achievement or they may think they can
    only do things if an adult helps them. Sometimes you
    need to wait to be asked or you need to be busy doing
    something else, like getting the dinner, so that you are
    not always in your child's space.

4. Don't become pushy and over anxious! This is easy to
    say but when you are trying to help your child with
    skills and tasks which are normally the preserve of the
    classroom, it is easy to get over involved. Remember
    your child still needs a home life and to relax when they

are with you –"**little and often**" is a very good maxim for working with your child on literacy or numeracy practice.

There are two huge bonuses which will arise from taking these tips on board:

- You will develop a closeness with your child which might not otherwise have happened

- Your child will mature and develop thinking strategies which are hugely beneficial in the working world and are likely to set them apart in a positive sense

Positive thinking strategies.

These were referred to above and they need a little space to explain what they are about and how they work. Once these techniques are mastered, they will become very useful to you in other areas too, such as talking to your child's teacher. The techniques come from psychological theories where it has been found that they can be very useful in life generally; you may have heard them referred to as emotional intelligence. So, let's explore the theory about how we think, it will be worth it!

As we grow up, we develop thinking patterns and a value system which in part comes from our parents. Some psychologists (Berne originally and then Stewart and Joines) developed a theory called Transactional Analysis which is about analysing the interactions between people, that is what they say to each other. They compartmentalised these reactions into three areas - the adult, parent or child zones.

Whether these transactions are positive or not, will depend on the circumstance.

They saw the **parent** state as being responsible for behaviours that were either **Nurturing** - Nurturing (positive) and Spoiling (negative) or **Controlling** - Structuring (positive) and Critical (negative). So, for example, if you are with your child, then talking to them with nurturing statements is appropriate but spoiling statements may not be, and when talking to another adult at work, neither would be appropriate.

The **Adult** state is the rationalising element but again, whilst it is appropriate to be rational and problem solving with another adult, your child does not want a rational approach when they have just fallen over and hurt their knee!

Finally, the **Child** state is separated into **Adapted** – Co-operative (positive) and Compliant/Resistant (negative). **Free** – Spontaneous (positive) and Immature (negative). To understand these, imagine you are at work, and you are receiving requests from your manager to undertake a certain project. It would be appropriate to respond cooperatively but not to be excessively compliant (because then you might not bring up real problems with the project which need to be ironed out before you begin work) or resistant. The acceptance that the manager is there to give you work is what makes it alright for you to operate in the child stance. Finally, imagine that you are out for a social event with your peers. You would want to have a good time and act in Child Free but you would not want to relinquish all controls in your behaviour and be immature as the results could be very damaging!

An understanding of these states and their effects can be very illuminating on your role with your child and those adults that you might meet in a support capacity, such as the child's teacher, the special educational needs specialist at school or the educational psychologist. (For more, look at the section on establishing an effective partnership with the school).

Let us concentrate here on your relationship with your child. The appropriate states are likely to be nurturing parent when you are looking after them, free child if you are out in the park or on an outing to a theme park for example, and adult if you are trying to jointly problem solve with them.

Behaviours such as shouting at them or encouraging learned helplessness or being over anxious are all negative parental states. This method of analysing your transactions with your child has another advantage. The bond between you and your child is an emotional one and it is easy to become over-emotional when you are trying to deal with all the feelings your child's dyslexia may cause. Using this analysis allows you to see the situation from a certain amount of distance, a bit like watching what is happening between you, from a camera mounted on the wall. This distanced analysis will be very helpful to you if you are in danger of an emotion getting in the way of finding good solutions to problems thrown up by the dyslexia.

Another significant point arising from Transactional Analysis is that it explains why we tend to set patterns for our children based on those set by our parents. Everything we instill in our children stays with them for life like a mantra. This can be very beneficial and may be a way of passing on wisdom to our children. However, if we pass on negative thinking patterns, such as "you'll never amount to anything" or "I've always failed at that" or "You can't expect to succeed with that because of your dyslexia", then inevitably this is not beneficial! Most parents would be horrified to learn that they had given their children such emotional baggage but often it happens without us even realising. What it implies for parents with dyslexic children is how important it is to instill positive messages to raise their child's self-esteem.

So how do we give our children positive thinking strategies? We use cognitive behaviour strategies. We need to teach them a series of questions to ask themselves to stop them jumping to negative conclusions. For example, your child might say, "John doesn't want to sit next to me in class because I can't read as well as him." Actually, there might be a whole host of reasons why John doesn't want to sit next to him or maybe John doesn't have a view on who he wants to sit next to and so on. So rather than your child jumping to this sort of conclusion, which puts them in a less positive position, we want to challenge this idea and also teach them to challenge such ideas for themselves. This is quite easy to do, provided you remember the strategy. Each time your child makes a point like this, go over these questions with them:

- What other reasons might be behind this?
- What evidence or facts have you to support any of your conclusions?
- How would you feel about any of these possibilities?
- What would you like to happen?

Obviously, you would need to phrase these questions in your own words and simplify it for younger children. However, what it does is:

- makes them challenge assumptions which it might not be in their best interests to hold
- starts to get them thinking about how they might control the situation
- begins the process of being assertive, i.e. not accepting passively the things that are happening to them
- identifies feelings and emotions so that you can discuss how they feel with them and how they can deal with those feelings

This may seem very technical and rather a formal way of helping your child. It does need practice as it is a skill and all skills have to be practised and learned. However, it is a very simple technique once you have mastered it and it can be very effective.

Choosing the best school for your child.

There are both state schools that have built up expertise in supporting dyslexic children and private schools that specialise in dyslexia teaching, and you will need to choose which you would prefer to send your child to. The B.D.A. is able to give you information about school choices and there are some schools who have achieved the coveted B.D.A. Dyslexia Friendly Quality Mark. It is also useful to look at Crested schools who provide significant support for those with a pronounced specific difficulty.

If there isn't a school in your area that provides dyslexia friendly teaching, then you may want to think about additional support for your child out of school hours. There are specialist teachers who are available to provide specialist dyslexia tuition privately. You can find one of these from the contact details provided in the last chapter. Alternatively, the B.D.A. has a new project called 'Children Will Shine' which is facilitating the setting up of workshops for children with dyslexia in schools. These are currently available in London and Manchester but with planning to extend their coverage to other areas. For further information on these centres contact **admin@bdadyslexia.org.uk**.

However, here we are going to concentrate on what you can do to assess whether the school you are considering is actually showing signs of expertise with teaching dyslexic pupils.

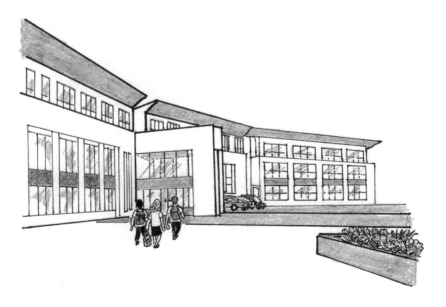

Mild to moderate dyslexia.

If the dyslexia is mild, then the current thinking is that the child is best supported in the mainstream classroom. The way of looking at this is that the dyslexic child processes information differently but all children have a preferred learning style and it is important that all learning styles are catered for, including the mildly dyslexic. Here are things to look for:

• Teaching is delivered in a multisensory way

This means that everything is taught using all the senses. So things are communicated verbally, in pictures or written material and wherever possible this is backed up by a tactile experience. An example of this would be where simple words in a foreign language are displayed around the room or on a board for the children to see (visual), they may sing songs about them (auditory) and they are encouraged to write them down or handle cards with the words printed on them (tactile).

You should also notice that there is good signage around the school and the classroom. This signage might be in words and accompanied by pictures. There is multisensory methodology being used throughout the whole school.

• It is a very well organised environment

This applies to being tidy and clearly having a place for things to be put away and, therefore, found later. It also applies to their systems, that these are well organised so that the pupils are clear about what happens and how things work there.

- Staff should be trained in dyslexia awareness and teaching strategies

You can ask how many staff and teaching assistants have been trained in dyslexia awareness. This will give you firm evidence of the school's commitment in this area. You could also ask for examples about how dyslexic children have been taught previously. You cannot expect to be given individual information on pupils which would be confidential, but the staff should be able to tell you about strategies that have been used successfully and what they have learned from this experience.

- The potential for rapport with staff

You should feel that there is potential to build up a good relationship and trust with your child's prospective teacher and the head teacher.

Moderate Dyslexia.

If your child is moderately dyslexic, then the same pointers apply to choosing their school above. However, in addition you may want to ask about the school's relationships with outside experts. It is likely in the case of moderate dyslexia that the child will need some remedial help outside the normal classroom activities.

The school may seek external advice from educational psychologists, speech and language therapists or specialist teachers, so you will want to know that they have on going and productive relationships with these contacts. You may prefer the school to have a Special Educational Needs Coordinator, Inclusion Manager or Additional Learning Needs

coordinator on the staff (not all schools have one on site.)
It is also worth asking if the SENCo is a dyslexia specialist as
some have other specialisms. Advice gained from an outside
contact would be recorded in the School Action Plus plan
(note these plans are being phased out from 2013). If your
child needs specific help, then it would not be unreasonable
to ask the prospective school for contact with other parents
in the same position so that they could make contact with
you. This would give you the chance to ask how things have
gone for their children at the school.

The provision for children with moderate dyslexia is not
entirely clear at the time of writing following the publication
of the Green Paper, 'From Aspiration to Success'.

It has been decided that statements, school action and school
action plus will be abolished. The aim of the paper is to
make the whole area of support for children with disabilities
less confrontational. However, plans for how children with
dyslexia will be supported in the future are not included.
Discussions with Government representatives suggest that
our children will be covered by the 'Achievement for All'
policies.

What matters most is that your child gets the support
they need. The best way to achieve this is to create a good
relationship with your child's school and see what support
they can offer. It is extremely likely though that you may
either have to supplement what is on offer with private
support or fight hard to get what your child needs. There
is undoubtedly an issue about the scarcity of resources in
this area.

Severe Dyslexia.

Severe dyslexia is covered by a variety of legislation and codes of practice which are summarised below. Whilst protection … remains, there are considerable changes being made to this system as described in the Green Paper which was launched in April 2011 and communicated in the Queen's speech in May 2012. At the time of writing, the Green Paper spelt out the new arrangements for combined health, care and education plans for disabled children. This does not seem to fit very well with the needs of children with severe dyslexia who do need an education plan, but probably don't need the health or care aspects. As details emerge of what will be on offer, the B.D.A. Helpline will be able to advise parents on what is available.

There is, however, specific legal protection for a severely dyslexic child.

Relevant Legislation.

The rights of children with disabilities are enshrined in the Equality Act (2010) which pulled together lots of previous legislation. These rights have been translated into what is needed to meet the legislation in an educational context. This gave rise to the Code of Practice 2001. The following describes what is available currently and then makes note of the changes to come under the new Green Paper.

Code of Practice 2001.

Dyslexia is to be found in paragraph 7:58 in an area of need headed 'Cognition and Learning'. If a dyslexic child has needs that cannot adequately be met, there may be a requirement for the protection of a Statement of Educational Need. Their procedures are a matter of law. The statement should clearly specify the provision necessary to meet each identified need (para 8:36/7). Provision should normally be quantified (e.g. in terms of hours of provision, staffing arrangements etc.), although there will be cases where some flexibility should be retained in order to meet the changing needs of the child concerned. It is now officially recognised that pupils should be involved in any plans made for them.

There are sections describing desirable practice in early years, primary and secondary provision. Three action steps are codified within a graduated approach:

* School Action;
* School Action Plus;
* The Statement.

In practice, what these mean is that the child with difficulties is first included with the school action plan. Under this, it is expected that their needs can be met in the classroom via the class teacher. If the child isn't progressing as anticipated after a period on School Action, they may be then transferred to School Action Plus. In this, the requirement to give them individual support is greater. For example, under School Action Plus, the child may receive some specific intervention which is delivered one to one by a teaching assistant working with them. If the child is significantly behind and not making progress, then it might be considered necessary to provide them with a Statement. You should note that in many areas, a child has to be 5 years behind and have multiple disabilities before statementing is considered necessary.

There are considerable changes planned to this system with consultation going on now. The proposed plan is to reduce the listing of the number of children currently on School Action and School Action Plus and to replace the Statement with a single Education, Health and Care Plan. If you would like to read more about this, the Green Paper is called "Support and Aspiration: A new approach to special educational needs and disability." It is available from the Department for Education at their website at **www.education.gov.uk**.

Under current arrangements, much of the responsibility for supporting children with dyslexia falls to the classroom teacher. Their role in this area was enshrined in the National Curriculum as follows:

National Curriculum Inclusion Statement.
Responding to pupils' diverse learning needs.

Teachers should take action to respond to pupils' diverse needs by:

- creating effective learning environments;
- securing their motivation and concentration;
- providing equality of opportunity through teaching approaches;
- using appropriate assessment approaches;
- setting targets for learning

Assessments and examinations.

When children approach tests or exams such as GCSEs, there is good provision for them through what are called Access Arrangements.

"Teachers must ….. make provision, where necessary, to support individuals or groups of pupils to enable them to participate effectively in the curriculum and assessment activities."

There are a very wide range of adjustments which may be put into place. These include things like working on a word processor if the child's handwriting is very poor or having a prompter if they are easily distracted and lose focus a lot. A longer list of these is provided later in the Unit about Older Children and public exams.

Parent Partnership Service (PPS).

By law, Local Authorities have been required for some time to set up a Parent Partnership Service although there is no national standards for PPS. The aim is to provide a range of services for parents whose children have SEN, in order to empower them to play an active and informed role in their child's education. This includes access to an Independent Parental Supporter for those parents who want one.

Whilst no specific model is included for a PPS, there has been a culture change and many schools are keen to encourage parents to participate through regular meetings with teaching and/or support staff. Typically, what is emerging is a series of meetings at least twice a year, which in some cases may be combined with the normal parent/teacher evenings. Clearly, in choosing a school for your severely dyslexic child you would want to ask about the partnership arrangements between parents and teachers.

Building good partnerships with your child's school and teachers.

Mutual objectives.

The aim is to build rapport with the school, and specifically, trust and good communications with your child's teachers. Just like any other relationships in life, it will depend on having two things

- the same objective
- the resources to meet each other's needs.

The objective should be that both you and the teachers want the best for your child and for them to develop to their full potential. However, sometimes this goes wrong in the detail. You will want your child to reach their maximum potential. The teachers may not agree with you about what their potential is. They may also hold other views on what your child needs to learn to become a well rounded and educationally successful individual. It is clear from this that very clear communication is required to navigate these waters!

The second point about resources is critical in schools where the current resource budget is stretched. It is a common scenario for the teacher to want to do something for your child but to be hampered by the lack of resources in terms of their budget or time. This means that many schools are having to make compromises and this can lead to invidious distinctions being made. It is crucial that we as parents consider the teacher's point of view. They have perhaps thirty individual children in their class, all with individual needs of some kind to address. Often for the parents to express their understanding of this, helps create the rapport and trust that the parent desires to achieve with their child's teacher.

Barriers.

There are two things that can get in the way of the parent and school forming a good relationship. The first is that communication will never be on an even platform. Members of staff inevitably have more power in this environment as they have the expertise and position of authority. This can have two effects. Firstly, the parent who feels consciously underpowered in this situation may respond more aggressively than they intended. Secondly, the professional may wield their power unwisely or unconsciously. Neither is going to improve the communications process so it is wise for both parties to be aware of the dangers. It can also be a good idea for you to take someone with you to a formal meeting at the school. This could be a relative, a close friend or a Parent Partnership Volunteer. This will help restore equity in the power balance and also this person may be less emotionally involved and able to remember the detail of the conversation (or make notes for you).

Secondly, the parent was also once a school child themselves and all the frustrations or negative things that happened to them in the past have the potential to be stirred up like ghosts when they come to talk to staff. We can use transactional analysis, which was discussed earlier, to consider what happens in this circumstance and can anticipate that the parent may respond in their "child" state

when that is inappropriate and the teacher may go into their "parent" state which is also inappropriate. Either person acting in an inappropriate state will draw a response from the other that is definitely not positive!

The key to managing all this is to ensure that any transactions with the school are assertive. This means that they are neither passive nor aggressive but rational and based on joint problem solving (from the "adult" stance). Assertiveness rests on the proposition that both parties are equal and that this is respected in all transactions. It can be helpful to follow the assertive process which is:

- State what you want to happen and how you feel
- Get the other party to state what they want to happen and what they feel
- Agree jointly on a way forward.

Good meeting skills.

All meetings are improved by some simple processes and school meetings are no exception. Prepare before you go by creating a simple list or agenda of the things you want to discuss. Agree this list with the teacher first. This will avoid distractions and help you cover all the things that you want to be included. Also agree with the teacher how long you both think you need for the meeting so that you are able to concentrate on the matter in hand and quality time is provided for it. Make sure you have agreed any decisions you reach and at the end of the meeting, it is quite a good idea to confirm them in summary so that there is no confusion afterwards.

Helping your child develop coping mechanisms.

Quite apart from literacy problems, your child may well have difficulty organising themselves. It is very important that you help them to develop coping strategies for planning and organisation. They will need to learn some specific strategies, such as the items in this comprehensive list. Some of these are strategies you can teach your child but others may be best taught by your child's specialist tutor.

Memory strategies:

- concept mapping
- writing instructions down - always carrying a notebook/organiser

Organisation:

- concepts of time
- planning
- previewing
- contingency planning

Prioritising:

- to do lists
- timetables
- goal setting
- task analysis
- time management
- reviewing

Tools to help your child organise themselves:

There are lots of useful resources, often found around the house already that can really make a difference to getting organised:

- a dictaphone
- electronic organisers
- alarm clocks/mobile phones (for reminders)
- diaries/filofax
- wall charts/planners
- time management software
- urgent/important trays (to distinguish what needs to be prioritised)
- colour coded files (so you can find them quickly)
- post it notes (as memory aids)
- concept mapping software

Auditory strategies:

- taking notes effectively and easily
- skimming/scanning techniques
- visualisation skills for instructions
- concept mapping as a form of note taking
- planning presentations
- use the facility on the mobile phone for messages and key things to remember
- highlight important points in documents

- look at the summary and conclusions first when reading a report
- Look at who has written the document and for what purpose
- Use tape recorder/Dictaphone to make short notes
- Using colour coding/highlighters
- Get instructions/information broken down into small pieces
- Draw a process chart of important work processes or information/instructions
- Use presentation software for presentations

Visual strategies:
- Check lighting and location of workstation
- Use Dyslexia Friendly Style Guide for printed material (from B.D.A. website)
- Change paper colour to a pastel shade
- Change fonts to sans serif and at least size 12
- Change screen background colour
- Check out helpful apps for a mobile phone that help
- Use text to speech software such as "Text Help"
- Use speech to text software such as "Dragon Naturally Speaking"
- Draw concept maps to help you remember
- Highlight important information
- Get others to check any written work
- Read right to left to check for errors

- Get eyes checked for coloured overlays/lenses
- Use writing frames/proformas/planning
- Use bullet points
- Teach your child to edit their work, think COPS (capitals, organisation, punctuation, spelling)

Personal strategies:

Your child will be putting more effort into their learning and concentration than their peers, so it is important to avoid stress.

Help them to:

- take regular breaks
- eat properly
- drink plenty of water
- utilise a mentor
- set clear goals that are achievable
- learn relaxation techniques
- increase IT support
- use a stress ball (particularly to aid concentration)
- praise/reward themselves for good work
- review their work regularly

Teach your child to:

- understand themselves and how they learn most effectively
- use workspace for homework effectively

- find a quiet space for work needing concentration
- use signs on the desk or bedroom door if they are trying to concentrate
- use earplugs to block any noise
- break down tasks into manageable chunks
- be realistic in what they can achieve in a given time
- take regular exercise
- learn time management skills
- do the hardest work when they are at their best (morning/afternoon/evening)
- learn to support peers as well as seeking support for themselves
- allow them to be creative at finding solutions when things aren't working
- develop assertiveness skills
- develop anger management skills

You may be able to help them to develop some of these skills and approaches yourself but find out which of these are likely to be addressed in school. Here are some specific activities you can do which will naturally develop some of the aptitudes listed above.

- Have a lesson and homework timetable visible at home and check it each evening with your child
- Establish routines with your child, which includes meal breaks, homework periods, story time etc. This helps the child remember to do things by association of ideas.

- Help your child to acquire learn time management skills by prioritising what needs to be done urgently and what can be planned to be done later.

- Help your child to learn how to pack their school bag and help prepare a packed lunch etc. (One way of learning to take everything you need with you is to leave a note in a shoe!)

- Keep a good stock of pencils, pens etc in case their own get left behind or forgotten

- Buy envelope files and clear plastic wallets and encourage your child to organise their work so that they don't have to rely on their working memory to find things.

Helping your child to become literate and numerate.

It is very easy to say but try not to get over anxious about your child's literacy needs. All children learn at different rates and success may not happen as quickly as you would like but even though you may continue to worry about it, provided your child is getting regular practice and is using the channels they prefer to absorb information, they will eventually learn at the right pace for them. However, there are things which you can do to support them and if you can be confident and relaxed, you will both enjoy these activities.

Reading.

Reading is about picking up ideas from the printed page. An effective and enjoyable way to initiate an interest in reading is to look at picture books and discuss what ideas are being communicated by the pictures. There are now a good range of books for all ages which have beautiful illustrations and very little text. You may find that magazines of holiday destinations, the National Geographic journal, or magazines linked to particular hobbies, have lovely photographs that communicate all sorts of ideas and offer good opportunities for discussion. This activity will encourage an interest in the printed word, will show the link between finding out about places and events, as well as teaching research skills and increasing your child's vocabulary. It is particularly suitable for older children who find reading more difficult and need age appropriate reading material.

When the time comes for reading practice remember that little and often is the best approach. If possible, try to find time every day to read together stories that you will both enjoy. This should be a combination of you reading aloud and your child reading to you, perhaps from a school reading book, but this should not take more than ten minutes. For a change or with more difficult material, try paired reading, where you read a sentence (or paragraph) and then your child reads the next and so on. Make sure you both read aloud as this works on both visual and auditory senses. (Research has shown that children learn much faster from hearing their own voice reading words than someone else's voice). It is always easier to learn if you are relaxed and enjoying yourself, so look for humorous books, especially those with cartoon strips, which will still encourage practice but make you both laugh.

As your child gets older, continue to take an interest in anything they read. If they have a set text, read it yourself so that you can talk knowledgeably about it with them. Your interest will help motivate your child to persevere because they will think that if you are interested in it, it must be worth reading. Usually it doesn't take long to read set books and you might discover something really interesting in it for yourself anyway. Continue to read to your child later than you might with a child who discovers reading for themselves at an earlier age.

It can be worth asking your child's teacher if there is work for the following day which requires quiet reading and if it is possible to have it the day before so that you can go over it with your child in advance. This can be very helpful in preventing your child from feeling that they are out of step with their peers but it will depend on how manageable it will be in practice for the teacher to arrange to send home.

Spelling.

The number of words that we use regularly is relatively small. These are the ones to concentrate on when helping your child learn common words for spelling. They don't have to learn *all* the words in the English language fortunately! There are lots of games which you can play together as a family that encourage the acquisition of accurate spelling. These include:

- "I spy" - where you have to guess the word from the initial letter. You could always extend this by including the next letters until the word is guessed.

- Scrabble - though this is quite a difficult game for a diffident speller, so perhaps add an extra rule such as "only up to 4 letter words can be used".

- Pairs - where you create pairs of words on the word processor to be printed out and then cut up to separate them. They are shuffled and spread out upside down. You take turns to turn them over and the winner is the one with the most pairs. This game also encourages the development of visual memory skills too.

- Word hunts - which you can buy in puzzle books.

- For young children, you can create road signs (with words and symbols) on card or the sides of boxes and they can be encouraged to drive their pedal car or bike around them. You can make a STOP/GO sign which you can use to play with them when they are on their bike. This is a valuable game for introducing children to the concept of a world where words matter.

When you need to help your child with learning spelling lists from school, remember again to keep it the activity short. Use a multisensory approach, look at the word (visual), say it (auditory), write the word, trace it with your child's finger, or walk around the house spelling the words in different places (tactile). You could even chalk the words on the drive or path and play a form of hopscotch to help it get into your child's long term memory! Then ask your child to repeat it without help, praise them if they get it right but just pass on if it is wrong and repeat the learning process.

For difficult words you could make up a rhythm or rhyme or a mnemonic. (Mnemonic comes from the Greek word for memory and can be anything which is an aid to memory). The more off beat, zanier or larger than life you make the idea - the better! For example, if I wanted to remember the spelling of "toad" I would write it across the back of a picture of a great big, ugly looking greeny/brown toad to help me remember.

Colour and repetition also work well. To learn spellings or later to revise facts, write them on different pieces of highly coloured paper and put them around where the child normally goes so that his/her eyes rest on them without any effort such as on their bedside table, next to their cup or near the loo! This makes memorising easy as it just happens naturally.

Writing.

1. Dyslexic children sometimes have problems with handwriting.

When learning to read, children first have to match the shape of the word on the page with the sound it makes. Then, when it comes to writing, they have to recreate that shape onto paper. For children with dyslexia, decoding these patterns and making these links can often be very difficult. As a result, they frequently fail to develop the automatic flow of writing which will help them to express themselves clearly and easily in writing.

Again, little and often is the key here. Copying out lines of sample text onto lined paper is extremely boring (no wonder it was used as a punishment in schools in the past!). If at all possible, try to build writing practice into normal life.

For example, make a shopping list together, where your child gets to add three things they would like to buy to eat. Or you could prepare a menu for a special meal. Write labels for photographs from a holiday or to record something to do with a hobby. Writing short letters to apply for "free stuff" is another possibility which encourages both a small amount of writing and learning how letters are set out, but is also fun to do. If you know and understand your child's interests, you will be able to think of lots of ideas for short writing projects that will hold their attention. If these do not work, then bribery might be the answer. Offer a reward of a small treat if the amount of handwriting practice you have agreed with their teacher is completed.

Bear in mind that if your child is approaching puberty, then they will start to grow rapidly and undergo lots of changes. If they haven't learned to write neatly yet, take the pressure off them. The facts are that they won't learn to improve their writing significantly whilst all this change is going on and it may be better to concentrate on learning to touch type. It is worth pointing this out to your child's teacher if they are still concentrating on handwriting skills.

2. It is recommended that children learn the continuous cursive style.

Typically, when first learning to write, children 'print' their letters. They then move on to 'joined up' writing at a later stage. For children with dyslexia, learning two styles of handwriting can add an extra layer of difficulty and cause confusion. It is, therefore, much more helpful if a young child can learn to use a single system of handwriting right from the start.

The most widely recommended handwriting style is called continuous cursive. The most important feature is that each letter is formed without taking the pencil off the paper – and consequently, each word is formed in one, flowing movement.

The key advantages to this system are:

- By making each letter in one movement, children's hands develop a 'physical memory' of it, making it easier to produce the correct shape;

- Because letters and words flow from left to right, children are less likely to reverse letters which are typically difficult (like b/d or p/q);

- There is a clearer distinction between capital letters and lower case;

- The continuous flow of writing ultimately improves speed and spelling.

3. Practising continuous cursive handwriting.

If you wish to practise handwriting with your child, it is advisable to use a recommended teaching resource. This will show you exactly how to form the letters and how best to practise them. You can get details on what is available either from the B.D.A.'s publication list but also from the National Handwriting Association. It is worth paying attention to a few basics, such as:

Paper: It is a good idea to use lined paper. At the earliest stages, you can use double lines to show the correct size of ascenders and descenders. Lines should be well spaced to start with – e.g. 10mm apart – gradually reducing to single lines about 5mm apart. You can buy paper which has coloured lines to write inside or you can make this yourself with a highlighter pen and a ruler. The aim is for the child to write the curves within the coloured area and ascenders go up above it. Using this simple strategy some children, especially those who may have a visual difficulty, experience an immediate improvement in the tidiness of their writing and legibility.

Posture: Make sure that the chair and desk are at the correct height. Your child's back should be straight with their feet resting on the floor. A right-handed child should have their book slanted to the left. For a left-handed child the book should be slanted to the right.

Implements: It is best to use a standard well sharpened HB pencil. With very young children, you may wish to use a chunky triangular pencil to encourage the correct grip. As children get older and more confident, they can move on to a fountain pen or a special handwriting pen. You should avoid using ballpoint pens for handwriting exercises.

Finally, don't feel too bad if your child just refuses to do any of this at home. They will be busy learning these strategies at school where one of the greatest motivators is peer pressure.

You need to remember that home is a special place and they may not want to do more of the same with you.

Computing.

If you can afford it, a basic computer will be invaluable for your child. This can be used for doing homework and research and there are specific packages that are designed to help with reading, spelling and organisation strategies. Although information on some of these packages is given below, many resources are more suitable for use in school where the cost can be is spread.

Word processing is likely to be essential for the dyslexic adult, so getting started early on learning to type properly is vital. There are several good typing software packages available and many have been developed for the dyslexic learner, such as Touch Type Read and Spell.

You can also check out whether your computer can use sound. If you can hear sounds on CD-ROMs, then your computer can support synthetic speech. You can then use Natural Reader which is freely available on the web or buy a text reading programme such as Claro or textHELP:Read and Write 2000, which is compatible with Microsoft Word and can be set up to read out loud as you type, or to read the whole document. You child can also use it to copy from web pages and read out the text.

In addition to standard software, there are a number of packages specifically for help with dyslexia. These include:

- Penfriend for word prediction, Clicker and Text help

British Dyslexia Association Membership.

The British Dyslexia Association offers a wide range of membership options. This includes individual, organisational and local dyslexia associations.

By becoming a member of the B.D.A. you will be entitled to a host of benefits, including:

- Dyslexia Contact magazine.

- E-newsletter 3 times per year.

- Discount on B.D.A. conferences.

- Discount on B.D.A. open training events.

- Consultation on key policy issues.

- Discounted price the Dyslexia Journal.

- Option to receive a Dyslexia Handbook each year.

Full details of the various types of membership and how to join can be found on our website, **www.bdadyslexia.org.uk/membership.html**. Alternatively, you can contact the Membership team on 0845-251-9003.

- Textease, Talking First Word, Clicker 5, Word with text to speech program, Portable Writing Aids
- Inspiration, Kidspiration enable concept maps to be created, and Writing Frames and planners are available to use onscreen
- Hand held spellcheckers, such as Franklin Spellmaster and talking calculators are also helpful.

New computer models are always being developed and software is constantly updated so it is possible that you might want to buy more as it becomes available. There follows a list of features which you should look for when choosing such software. The software should have:

- options of full speech support on content, menus and help features
- clear, spoken instructions that can be repeated or paused
- opportunities to review and repeat
- options to alter format – background, font, font size and colour
- clear uncluttered screens
- written text in a clear readable format and font
- clear images that can be easily identified
- easy navigation with clear icons for accessing tools, menus or onscreen help
- tracking facilities where appropriate – time taken, tasks attempted or completed
- options available to meet individual learning preferences

- options for differentiated levels or activities, where appropriate
- full speech support for word processed text, spellcheckers and word banks
- option of printed reports where appropriate
- spellcheckers with speech support and definitions
- options for text highlighting with speech when selected
- additional access options if required (e.g. switch control).

The B.D.A. has a website at **www.bdatech.org.uk** where constantly updated information on IT is available. You can now browse or buy software from the B.D.A. shop. This is available by going to **www.bdadyslexia.org.uk**.

Private Dyslexia Tuition.

You may decide that the best option for you and your child is to buy in some trained support for literacy and numeracy.

B.D.A. has a list of specialist teachers with B.D.A. accreditation. Many of our Local Dyslexia Associations hold a list of specialist dyslexia teachers working in their area. There are specialist dyslexia teaching centres in different parts of England and Wales. The B.D.A. publishes a list of those which are organisational members. PATOSS (Professional Association for Teachers of Students with Specific Learning Difficulties) has a national tutor index list available and is also able to arrange insurance for teachers.

The B.D.A. has initiated a project to provide out of school workshops for children with dyslexia in areas where parents may find it difficult to pay for private tuition. The project called 'Children Will Shine' is currently running workshops in Southwark, and Barnet in London and in East Manchester and is about to commence new groups in Peterborough and a further group in Manchester. The children are supported by a team of teaching assistants led by a specialist teacher. They focus on literacy, and touch typing and aim to improve self-esteem. All the teaching is dyslexia friendly. For more details of this, contact **admin@bdadyslexia.org.uk**.

If you are aiming to find a private tutor then it is advisable to establish ground rules from the start. Both parties should satisfy themselves that the tutor is able to meet the child's needs and that they have a good rapport.

The following information may be useful as a guide to help you choose a tutor.

Specialist Teaching.

- Teachers should be able to produce qualifications with dates, including their Department for Education and Skills number.

- Details of their teaching experience supporting children with dyslexia are essential.

- One of the following specialist dyslexia teacher training qualifications is preferable: (See SpLD ,Specific Learning Difficulties, courses accredited by B.D.A.)

  - SpLD Certificate qualification for either primary, secondary or adult levels. The level accredited should be indicated. (Holders of this diploma may be eligible to apply for ATS (Approved Teacher Status from B.D.A.).

  - SpLD Diploma which accredits all three levels. (Holders of this diploma may be eligible to apply for AMBDA (Associate Member of B.D.A.).

- Teachers should be regularly updating their knowledge with courses, seminars and conferences etc. They may be members of other specialist groups such as PATOSS. They should hold a current assessing or teaching certificate which you could ask to see.

- It should be possible for teachers to produce references on request which would be applicable to teaching a child of the same age

You will also need to consider the following detailed criteria:

- Would a multisensory structured programme such as Hickey, Alpha to Omega, etc., be used to develop literacy skills ?

- Is it appropriate for the specialist teacher to be familiar with the National Curriculum, or with particular GCSE syllabuses?

- Would study skills need to be taught?

- Would ICT be available and/or beneficial?

- Are there recommendations from assessments by either a Chartered Educational Psychologist or a Specialist Teacher to work from?

- Would the teacher be suitably qualified to make an assessment either for their own teaching purposes or for provisions for examinations such as GCSE (SpLD Diploma holders only)?

- Would the teacher be required to write reports or be prepared to attend meetings at school or to liaise with the school?

- Clarify the frequency of the lessons, a suitable venue and an appropriate lesson time. It is possible for a school to approve absence for an education activity including:

"Franchised pupils receiving part of their tuition at another location while remaining under overall supervision of the home/school (i.e. a flexible arrangement short of formal dual registration). This can include special tuition for dyslexic children and sick children being taught at home but remaining on roll." DfES, formerly DfEE, Circular 10/99.

- Would you want to observe the lessons?

- Would homework be set with guidelines for your assistance?

Fees and Conditions.

- It needs to be established whether the lessons will be on an individual or group basis.

- Duration of lessons, fees and payment arrangements need to be agreed.

- You need to negotiate cancellation fees or additional charges for materials.

- Agreement is needed concerning the frequency of verbal or written reports and whether these would be chargeable. Bearing in mind that progress should be reviewed regularly, e.g. termly or at six monthly intervals with reports.

- Insurance for the teacher would be advisable. B.D.A. and PATOSS are able to arrange this.

- Certificates confirming police checks (CRBs) should be obtained. Those teachers employed by a DfE registered (state) school should have this already in place.

- Both verbal and written references should be readily available.

Useful Contacts.

Applications for ATS and AMBDA can be made to the B.D.A..
Tel: Administration 0845-251-9003.
Email: **accreditation@bdadyslexia.org.uk**

Department for Education (DfE)
Web: **www.education.gov.uk/**

PATOSS: The Professional Association of Teachers of Students with SpLD
Web: **www.patoss-dyslexia.org**

Summary.

In this chapter we looked at the specific things you, and sometimes, only you, can do to help your child. These priorities included:

- Building your child's self esteem
- Determining the best strategy for your child's education
- Building good partnerships with your child's school and teachers
- Helping them develop coping mechanisms which minimise any weaknesses
- Helping them become literate and numerate

Chapter 4 – Older Children and Teenagers.

It can be difficult to help your older dyslexic child directly as, with all teenagers, they want increasingly to become independent of their parents. However, there are still some things you can do which will make a real difference. These include knowing what's available regarding exams and practical help for learning to drive and passing a test.

Changing Schools.

Change nearly always provokes anxiety unless we have sought it out. Consequently you should not be surprised if you or your child is anxious about the thought of changing schools. It will inevitably mean that there will be a new situation for both you and your child to get used to. You may have been very successful in building up a positive relationship with the current school and dread the fact that you will have to start again. Your child may be concerned about practical things like knowing where things are and getting to know new teachers. However, the fact that you have coped so far, is an indicator that you can do so again. The best thing you can do is to prepare as much as possible for the change.

Most primary schools have well developed relationships with the secondary schools they feed into. Talk to your child's teacher at least a year ahead of the change and find out what they think is best for your child. Investigate what support systems the different schools have, if you have a choice. Then you can arrange to visit them well ahead of the time you have to make a choice. Look again at the earlier section in this book on signs that the school is good with dyslexic pupils, to see what evidence you can gather before making your choice

When you have made a shortlist, talk again to your child's teacher and see what specific practices and procedures they have with those schools to prepare for a smooth transition. They may be able to offer a handover system to your child's prospective new teacher, explaining the child's strengths and weaknesses, what has been done so far in remedial help and what their preferred learning styles are. Most schools arrange for the transferring children to visit several times. If possible, see if via the SENCo or the new teacher, you can arrange with them that during these visits, a particular member of staff introduces themselves to your child so that they have a familiar and friendly face for their first few days. Some schools offer summer schools and a few have a specific individual programme of support for children who for a variety of reasons, may find the transition more stressful. They may also arrange for your child to have a buddy, an older child within the school who will act as a mentor and support them until they have found their feet.

When the decision has been made, it would be advisable for you to help your child with organisation by carrying out several dummy runs to the school beforehand. This will help to normalise the routine and make the journey there a familiar event.

In the first couple of weeks while your child is settling in, try to be there for them when they return each day even if it's in the background making the tea! Even though they may not tell you, when life is a bit tougher, it's when they really need your love and support. Knowing you're there if they want to talk to you (even if they don't actually do so), being around and just chatting about everyday events, enjoying meals and watching television together can make a lot of difference and reduce stress levels considerably. So organising your life in advance for this can be very beneficial.

Homework Tips.

1. Introduction.

Homework can be a frustrating and upsetting experience for dyslexic children and their parents on a daily basis. Below are some tips to help make homework a more profitable experience.

First of all, remember: the purpose of homework is to practise something that your child is already familiar with. If homework is too difficult, you should discuss this with the child's teacher. Don't allow your child to become frustrated because homework tasks are beyond their skills or take too long. Setting smaller amounts of work and/or allowing extra time will often help.

2. Establishing a routine.

Develop a daily homework routine. A written or visual plan put in a prominent place is ideal. It should include a particular place set aside for homework and an agreed plan as to what happens after arrival home from school. It should also be flexible enough to take into account after-school activities.

The homework place needs to be as quiet as possible, with a cleared space for work and items required at hand e.g. pens, pencils, rubber, books. The kitchen table is suitable if close supervision is required at busy times.

Work out the best time for your child to do their homework. Keep in mind that your child may be very tired after school – they have had to work harder than their peers because of their dyslexia. They may need a break and a snack before starting homework.

Daily reading is essential, as lots and lots of practice is required for students with dyslexia to develop and master literacy skills. Read aloud with your child when they are becoming frustrated. This helps them to understand and enjoy what they are reading and it still helps them to learn. Your child can also read along with books on tape or a CD.

3. Getting started.

Chunk homework tasks into manageable portions. The dyslexic student can become discouraged when faced with large amounts of work. Give breaks between tasks. Encourage your child to produce work of quality rather than rushing to finish it.

Go over homework requirements to ensure your child understands what to do. Read instructions aloud when you know it is hard for them to decode accurately. If necessary, practise the first example or two with them.

Help your child to generate ideas for writing tasks and projects before they start work. If necessary, revise vocabulary that they may need. Sometimes you may need to help them to develop a writing plan or a concept map.

Encourage them to present work using their personal strengths - for example, they could use pictures if they are good at art. When necessary and appropriate, scribe for your child so that they can get their ideas on paper more accurately whilst they are still fresh.

4. Checking and monitoring work.

Help your child to learn editing, self-monitoring and checking skills so they can go over their own work more independently as they get older. For example, a simple process like COPS can be helpful when proof reading work:

C = Capitals.
O = overall appearance.
P = punctuation.
S = spelling.

Encourage your child to use the computer (for tips on this see earlier section on computing).

If they are slow to complete work, encourage them to use a timer and see how much work they can complete in five minutes. But remember that if homework is regularly taking too long or is too difficult, you should discuss this with the relevant teacher.

Give your child lots of praise as they complete homework tasks. Be specific about what they have done well.

5. Organisation.

Help them to develop a comprehensive, written homework plan. Include revision of subjects as well as the set homework tasks. Monitor the time spent on homework and also the results.

Encourage your child to keep their school notes and work together in folders so they don't get lost or damaged. Organise notes into subjects, and ensure that they are filed regularly. Colour coding of subjects can greatly assist organisation and planning.

If students are not getting their homework down accurately, arrange for them to check with someone in the same class at the end of the day or ask teachers to give them written homework instructions for more complex tasks.

Liaise with teachers regularly to check that students are completing both homework tasks and classwork appropriately and are handing in work promptly at school.

Check that your child is bringing the correct books and equipment to school each day. Develop a visual or written plan if this is an area of difficulty.

6. Study skills.

Make sure that your child has effective plans for approaching tasks like essay writing and coursework. Talk to the school's SENCo or subject teachers about these. There are also some specific tips on exam preparation below.

Build up independent work skills in your child and problem solving strategies when they are "stuck" or not sure of how to tackle homework. For example, get your child to think about several different ways they could complete the task correctly. They can also think about who they can ask for help when they have tried other strategies and are still confused.

Examinations and assessments.

Exam periods are testing not just of the subject matter under review but also for organisational ability, memory skills and stress management. These are all you can help your child with.

Find out when exams and assessments are taking place and put them in your diary or make up a multi coloured planner where you can both see it is useful for getting organised.

You can also help your child make up a small project plan for revision, helping them with time management, revision periods and target dates for completing topics and course work. Help them to learn that they may not find cramming a comfortable way to revise because it relies on the use of working memory and can also be physically very tiring.

Devising concept maps, putting revision notes onto CDs, iPods or other recording devices, or making colourful or zany representations may all help to fix things in the memory. Concept maps are also a very useful way to tackle previous exam questions without having to write out the whole answer. They are also a brilliant way to organise material to answer questions and to plan essays.

There is almost always a technique to understanding exam questions and realising what you need to do. Reading out exam questions and discussing what is required will help your child learn this technique and also any specific exam vocabulary that they might not know.

If your child has severe dyslexia, they may be entitled to additional time in examinations. This is usually up to 25% extra time. The exam board will want to be satisfied that this is a genuine need and so is likely to ask for copies of assessments by qualified staff. You can ask your school or college about this but here is some outline information about the different assessments.

National Curriculum.

Assessments (known informally as SATs) are administered at the end of certain Key Stages. Notification is required for extra time and other arrangements.

If your child's school is a Local Authority (LA) school and it wants to make special arrangements for them, then it must notify an LA representative who monitors the situation. Non-LEA schools have to contact QCA. An Educational Psychologist's assessment is not needed for special arrangements for these tests.

The rules for these adjustments tend to be updated every year. For the most up to date information, see **www.qca.org.uk/**

Common Entrance examinations.

Special arrangements are a matter for negotiation with the destination school.

GCSE, GCE "A" levels and GNVQ examinations.

The aim of all adjustments is to provide access to individuals who would otherwise be treated less favourably than other candidates by reason of their impairment or disability. Schools and colleges, therefore, have to be very careful in the assessment of the individual's difficulties so as not to either unfairly disadvantage or advantage the candidate with dyslexia or any other disability.

What is available as an adjustment (known as an access arrangement) is slightly different every year (as technology and procedures are subject to change. The current menu of access arrangements includes the following:

- extra time up to 25%
- supervised rest breaks
- readers/computer readers
- read aloud
- scribes/voice input systems
- word processors
- transcripts
- prompters
- oral language modifier

- live speaker for pre-recorded exam components
- sign language interpreters
- practical assistants
- alternative accommodation
- bilingual translation dictionaries
- braillers
- colour naming by invigilators for the colour blind
- coloured overlays
- coloured/enlarged papers
- exemptions
- modified papers
- separate invigilation from the centre
- CCTV, low vision/magnifier, OCR scanners, amplification equipment

Some adjustments can be provided by the school on the recommendation of a specialist teacher who will have carried out some tests, for example, on speed or legibility of writing.

For more advanced adjustments, the exam boards may require a current assessment report from an Educational Psychologist or from a teacher with specialist qualifications for identifying, assessing and teaching pupils with dyslexia. Schools may be required to pay the LAs for such assessments. The report may not have to be submitted, but must be available if required.

Word-processed coursework is acceptable from all candidates, though some coursework and papers for some examination boards must be hand-written. Exam boards are unlikely to consider applications from candidates who have not used work processing in mock exams (as it is meant to represent the way the pupil normally works).

You can request the relevant booklets with guidance as follows:

GCE, VCE, GCSE & GNVQ. Regulations and Guidance relating to Candidates with Particular Requirements. Issued by the Joint Council for Qualifications. Available from the awarding bodies including:

Assessment & Qualification Alliance (AQA) Manchester
Tel: 0161-953-1180

Assessment & Qualification Alliance (AQA) Guildford
Tel: 01483-506-506

Edexcel
Tel: 0870-240-9800
Web: **http://www.edexcel.org.uk/**

OCR (Oxford, Cambridge & RSA)
Tel: 024-7647-0033
Web: **http://www.ocr.org.uk/**

Joint Council for Qualifications (JCQ)
Web: **http://www.jcq.org.uk/**

Welsh Joint Education Council (WJEC)
Tel: 02920265000
Web: **http:/www.wjec.co.uk/**

You will need to discuss your individual case with your child's school or college.

Applications to the Examination Board, with the required evidence, must be made by the school in good time.

The school must be able and willing to implement the special arrangements, e.g. disable the spellchecker and supervise extra time in a separate room for those using computers.

Further and Higher Education.

Application for access arrangements can be made to City & Guilds, BTEC, RSA, and other professional assessment bodies. They all have web sites which should carry up to date information and you can find these websites through Google.

Apprenticeships have been a natural home for many youngsters with dyslexia where they may excel with their strengths in problem solving and creativity. To participate in the scheme, they will have to complete the Apprenticeship Award. As feedback to the Government suggested that employers were anxious to have a literate workforce, literacy, numeracy and ICT skills tests were inserted into the Transferable skills component of the Framework. These can create a barrier for the dyslexic young person. Access arrangements permit the use of assistive software to allow text reading and voice recognition software. However, apprentices have not always been fortunate enough to learn how to use assistive software. Neither have their teachers. Added to this, at the time of writing, the papers are not compatibly formatted for use with assistive software. There is a huge learning curve to contemplate for everyone concerned.

In addition, it is possible to get significant support for implementing reasonable adjustments into graduate studies.

The funding for this comes through the Disabled Student Allowance (D.S.A.) and is generally administered through Student Finance England, Student Finance Wales or the N.H.S.

The young person will need to have a current diagnostic report. It may be necessary to get a top up report done to bring it up to date. Following application, the young person will be notified of their need for a D.S.A. assessment. These are done by trained assessors and their task is to identify what reasonable adjustments the individual will need to mitigate their disability. Typically for a dyslexic young person, the recommendations will include specific assistive technology and training in how to use it. There is considerable pressure on the assessors during the late summer and early autumn when lots of individuals need to be assessed, equipment bought and training provided. Therefore, it is extremely advisable to ensure that the diagnostic report is ready in good time and that the application for D.S.A. is made as soon as is possible. In this way, the young person can start their graduate studies with appropriate adjustments and tutor support in place from the outset.

Driving and driving tests.

Your teenager may want to learn to drive. You can talk to them with the driving instructor and arrange for specific coping mechanisms. For example, if your teenager has difficulty telling left from right, a small sticker could be placed in the windscreen on one side to indicate which it is.

There are arrangements for special needs in driving tests. For the theory test, the system has the option for dyslexic candidates to listen to the test being read in English through a headset. Dyslexic candidates can also apply to have up to double the standard 40 minutes. You need to ask when you apply for the test. A letter or report from a professional should explain your reading ability, i.e. a teacher, a psychologist, or Local Dyslexia Association officer. You will have to phone again for a test date after the report has been processed.

The practical driving test now carries a test of independent driving. This can be particularly challenging to those with dyslexia. It is possible to have a diagram of the route from your driving instructor which can be helpful. It is generally not possible to use a satnav system during your test, although the D.S.A. will consider it in cases of very severe dyslexia. When the driving test has been passed, a satellite navigation system can be extremely useful. Some dyslexic drivers find they cannot read the road signs giving directions at speed and they may find maps difficult to follow.

Summary.

In this chapter, we have looked at subtle ways of helping older children. These included:

- How to organise homework

- Revision and exams

- Driving and driving tests

Chapter 5 – The British Dyslexia Association.

About the B.D.A.

The B.D.A. is a national charity with a vision of a dyslexia friendly society that will enable all dyslexic people to reach their potential.

Mission.

Our mission is to:

- influence for long lasting and sustainable change for the benefit of dyslexic people.

- provide impartial and objective advice and support to dyslexic people and those with whom they come into contact.

- set the standards for and accredit dyslexia knowledge and professional expertise.

- deliver innovative solutions which break new ground in the field of dyslexia.

- disseminate and share best practice regionally, nationally and internationally.

- promote research.

Products and Services.

In addition to influencing to achieve positive change for those with dyslexia, the B.D.A. has a number of products and services. These are briefly described below.

B.D.A. Helpline.

The B.D.A. has always offered advice, information and help to dyslexic people of all ages and in 1980 the national Helpline was set up.

Accredited by the Telephone Helpliners Association, the Helpline is now staffed by a Helpline Manager, three Helpline Coordinators and 14 volunteers. Our volunteers are a mix of specialist teachers, parents and professionals from all walks of life, responding to 12,000 calls and 4,000 emails annually from around the world. There is also a dedicated line for teachers offering an out of hours service on Tuesday and Wednesday evenings.

The calls our Helpline receives are split 50/50 between child and adult related queries. All calls are treated confidentially and the information, advice and signposting given by our Helpline is always impartial, empowering people to make choices.

The B.D.A. Helpline can be contacted on 0845-251-9002.

B.D.A. Membership.

The B.D.A. has three categories of membership – individuals, local dyslexia associations and organisations. Schools, parents and organisations can support the work of the B.D.A. and the local dyslexia associations by becoming members, through sponsorship, donations, fundraising or offering free use of premises for events and conferences.

Members benefit from a range of services from receipt of our "Contact" magazine to opportunities to develop for our professional members, or discounts for training and conference booking.

The B.D.A. Dyslexia Friendly Quality Mark.

The B.D.A. Dyslexia Friendly Quality Mark is a registered kite mark that is awarded to organisations that can prove their dyslexia friendly practices. A number of Local Authorities and schools and colleges have been awarded the Quality Mark, and in November 2009 the first private company successfully gained the award.

The B.D.A. is also working with four other European countries on a European Union funded project, "Dyslexia VETO", to use the Dyslexia Friendly Quality Mark in vocational, educational and training settings in those countries as well as in the UK (**www.dyslexia-veto.eu**).

B.D.A. Training.

The B.D.A. organises 500 training events per year. The training covers awareness of dyslexia, screening for dyslexia and providing reasonable adjustments for all audiences. They also run the only available accredited programme for workplace assessors who specialise in dyslexia. Current information on our training courses is shown on our website at **www.bdadyslexia.org.uk** under Training and Events.

B.D.A. Conferencing.

The B.D.A. organises a number of conferences throughout the year, with topics for educationalists and employers, and themes such as Music and Dyslexia, Inclusion and Technology, or Dyslexia in the Workplace. Our conferences are always very successful and feedback is positive and encouraging.

The British Dyslexia Association's 8th International Conference was held on **2–4 June 2011** at Harrogate International Conference Centre with the theme "Beyond Boundaries". The conference was chaired by Joel Talcott PhD, an internationally recognised researcher and Reader in Developmental Cognitive Neuroscience from Aston University. These conferences are held every 3 years.

Please visit **http://www.bdadyslexia.org.uk/courses-and-events/conferences.html** for further details of our International Conference and other conferences that are available throughout the year.

B.D.A. Research Projects.

The B.D.A. undertakes major pieces of research into dyslexia and its related conditions. Currently, we have two large research projects. The first is on Vocational Educational and Training Organisations where 3 colleges in 5 European countries are pursuing the award of the Quality Mark.

The second project is on multilingualism and dyslexia, and the B.D.A. is working with Bath Spa University to identify ways to screen and support those who are dyslexic and have English as an additional language.

Children Will Shine Project.

The B.D.A. has concerns about children whose family or carers cannot, for reasons of affordability, access private support for their dyslexic children. It has therefore, started a project promoting out of school workshops for children in parts of London and Manchester. For further information on this please see our website.

How to contact the B.D.A.

The British Dyslexia Association
Unit 8, Bracknell Beeches
Old Bracknell Lane,
Bracknell RG12 7BW

Helpline Tel: 0845-251-9002
Office Tel: 0845-251-9003
Fax: 0845-251-9005
Web Address and eshop: **www.bdadyslexia.org.uk**

B.D.A. is a company limited by guarantee
Registered in England no.1830587
Registered Charity no. 289243.